LOWRIDERS

MOTOR Mania

by Matt Doeden

Pete Salas, consultant, founder of Los Padrinos lowrider club, Saint Paul, Minnesota

Lerner Publications Company • Minneapolis

Lerner Publications Company
A division of Lerner Publishing Group
241 First Avenue North
Minneapolis, MN 55401 U.S.A.

Website address: www.lernerbooks.com

Library of Congress Cataloging-in-Publication Data

Doeden, Matt.
    Lowriders / by Matt Doeden.
        p.   cm. — (Motor mania)
    Includes bibliographical references and index.
    ISBN-13: 978–0–8225–6042–5 (lib. bdg. : alk. paper)
    ISBN-10: 0–8225–6042–9 (lib. bdg. : alk. paper)
    1. Lowriders—Juvenile literature. I. Title. II. Series.
TL255.2.D64 2007
629.28'72—dc22   20050380481

Manufactured in the United States of America
1 2 3 4 5 6 – DP – 12 11 10 09 08 07

Contents

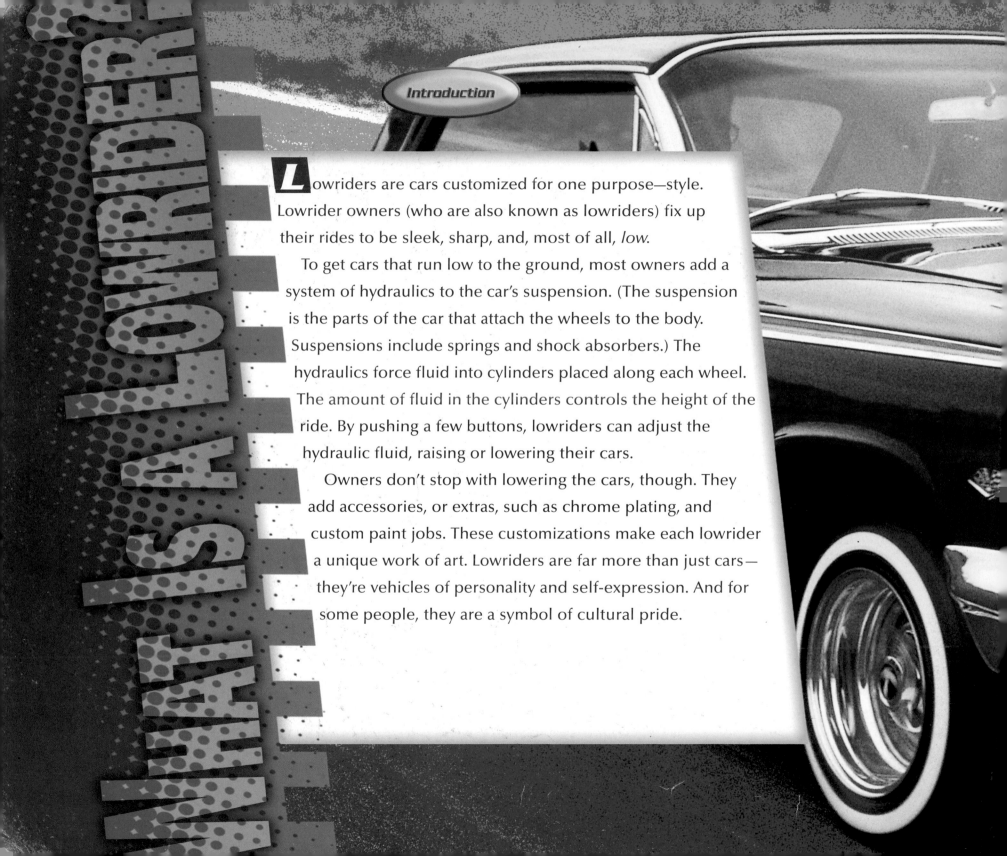

Introduction

Lowriders are cars customized for one purpose—style. Lowrider owners (who are also known as lowriders) fix up their rides to be sleek, sharp, and, most of all, *low*.

To get cars that run low to the ground, most owners add a system of hydraulics to the car's suspension. (The suspension is the parts of the car that attach the wheels to the body. Suspensions include springs and shock absorbers.) The hydraulics force fluid into cylinders placed along each wheel. The amount of fluid in the cylinders controls the height of the ride. By pushing a few buttons, lowriders can adjust the hydraulic fluid, raising or lowering their cars.

Owners don't stop with lowering the cars, though. They add accessories, or extras, such as chrome plating, and custom paint jobs. These customizations make each lowrider a unique work of art. Lowriders are far more than just cars— they're vehicles of personality and self-expression. And for some people, they are a symbol of cultural pride.

This 1963 Chevrolet Impala lowrider has a candy apple finish and chrome detailing (moldings, bumpers, grille, and rims).

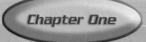

Chapter One

LOWRIDER HISTORY

*L*owriding grew out of the Mexican American culture of Southern California in the late 1930s and early 1940s. It was a difficult time for many Mexican Americans in the area. Many of them had recently come to the United States. And these were the years of the Great Depression. Jobs were scarce, and many people did not have much money. But despite the difficulties, cultural pride was high. Some Mexican Americans felt a strong need to express themselves and their pride in their culture. They worked to blend in with mainstream American culture, and they also wanted to keep their own identity.

During the 1930s, many Mexican Americans labored as farmworkers. They traveled from place to place in search of work, as this family is doing.

In Mexican American neighbor-hoods, called barrios, this self-expression first showed up in clothing. Many young men began wearing fancy "zoot suits," which were popular in the nation's big cities. They wore oversized coats and baggy, high-waist pants. Many of them showed off a hairstyle called a pompadour. They called themselves zoot-suiters, or pachucos.

Meanwhile, California had a booming car culture. Hot-rodding—customizing cars for racing—was becoming popular. The idea of a cool car was the "California rake," a sharp-looking car stripped down for racing.

Soon the sharp look of the pachucos spread to cars. Most pachucos were poor. They couldn't afford new cars or expensive new

Mexican American pachucos dance in the baggy, high-waisted pants of the popular zoot suit. (The men have taken off their loose-fitting, oversized coats.)

engine parts. They could never afford to keep up with the wealthier young men who were customizing their cars for speed. Instead, they focused on the look of their cars. One of the most popular changes was adding weight (usually bags of sand or cement) to the trunk. The extra weight made the car ride low. The bottom of the car almost touched the road. It was a cool look. These machines were the first lowriders.

The most popular model for these cars was the Chevrolet, especially the 1939 Chevy Deluxe. Early Chevys had everything lowriders wanted. They were sleek, durable, and affordable. Fords, another common car type, were also used as lowriders. But their bumpers had a dip in the center that got in the way when a car was lowered. So the Chevy ruled the barrios.

The lowriding fad quickly caught on.

Large, sleek cars like this 1953 Cadillac are still a popular choice for lowriders.

Soon Chevy lowriders were all over Los Angeles and other southwestern cities. The cars and their drivers were building a new cultural tradition. The lowriders were mixing their Mexican roots with the United States's mainstream car culture.

Birth of the Modern Lowrider

Through the late 1940s and early 1950s, lowriding grew in popularity. New models became favorites. They included the 1948 Chevy Fleetline, the 1950 Chevy hardtop, and the 1952 Mercury. Owners were finding new ways to customize their cars. Many added small tires. These were cheaper than big tires and also helped to lower the car. Drivers added fancy chrome bumpers and wheel rims. Brightly painted red rims were a hallmark of these early lowriders. Owners didn't pay much attention to the engines or the interiors, though. Lowriding wasn't about going fast. It was about riding low and slow and looking good.

This ultralow lowrider is a customized 1949 Buick Super Sedanette. Lowriders usually give their cars a name. This machine's name is *Fireball.*

But a problem was also developing. Government officials didn't want cars rubbing on the pavement and damaging streets. Many cities were passing laws about how low a car could ride. The laws said that the wheel rims had to be the lowest part of a car. No other part could hang lower than the rims. Any part lower than the rims would drag on the road if the car had a flat tire. Rough roads and potholes also

Torch Job

Some early lowriders used a cheap but permanent solution to lowering their cars. They used welding torches to cut and collapse their cars' metal springs. But getting all four wheels lowered to the same height was tricky. More important, the process couldn't be reversed. Torch jobs were cheap, but they often did more harm than good.

The smooth good looks of cars like this 1952 Mercury coupe (two-door car) make for great lowriders.

could be dangerous obstacles to the cars. Lowriders needed a new solution for lowering their cars. They needed a suspension system that could easily be adjusted. This would allow them the low, sleek look they wanted while keeping the cars legal. It would also give owners the ability to raise the cars for rougher roads.

In 1959 a Los Angeles man named Ron Aguirre finally came up with a solution. He had seen hydraulic systems on airplanes and delivery trucks. He knew how the systems worked. They lifted heavy objects by using pumps to force fluid into cylinders. Aguirre got some used hydraulic cylinders off an old World War II (1939–1945) plane. Then he installed them on his 1957 Chevrolet Corvette, which he'd named *X-Sonic*. The results were perfect. He could raise and lower the car as he pleased.

To test out his new system, Aguirre climbed into *X-Sonic* and headed to a

car show in Long Beach, California. He set the car to ride low, knowing that the police would be out in force. They would be looking to write tickets for anyone breaking the law with cars that were too low. Sure enough, he was pulled over as he approached the car show. But as the officer got off his motorcycle to measure the car, Aguirre used a switch to turn on the hydraulics and raise the vehicle.

The Chevy Fleetline *(above)* is one of the most popular lowrider bombs.

Below is a close-up of a lowrider hydraulic cylinder. The shiny chrome tube with the box-shaped nut on top is the hydraulic cylinder. The hoses coming out of the cylinder are filled with hydraulic fluid. The car's engine is to the left of the cylinder.

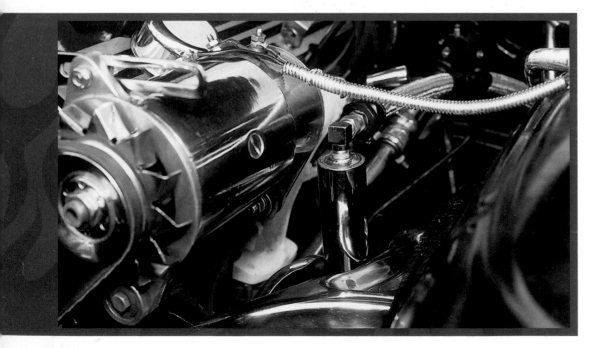

The officer was confused. He had been sure that *X-Sonic* had been too low to be legal. Aguirre told him that the car just looked lower than it really was. The officer could do nothing, so he let Aguirre go. As he walked away, Aguirre lowered the vehicle back down. The officer looked back one last time, completely confused.

The ability to raise and lower a car was a big change. *X-Sonic* was the talk of the show. Lowriding would never be the same.

New Horizons

At first, lowriding had been mainly a Southern California movement. But by the 1960s, it was spreading across the United States. Lowriders could be found more and more in southwestern states such as Texas, New Mexico, and Arizona.

Meanwhile, lowrider owners were organizing and forming clubs. Club members identified themselves by their cars' style and with fancy club plaques (name plates). But they still had a problem finding a place to cruise. New laws made showing off the cars on cruise strips difficult. Criminal gangs had also taken over many of the most popular streets and made cruising unsafe.

Frustrated, some clubs began organizing car shows. There, owners could show off their lowriders without fear of gangs or of being arrested. They could exchange tips and admire one another's hydraulic setups, paint jobs, and other customizations. The

Most lowriders have club plaques *(left)*.

most popular of these new shows was organized by a club of students that called themselves the Tridents. The Tridents Custom Car Show quickly grew into one of the biggest car events in Southern California. During the early 1960s, it was the place to be for lowrider fans.

Custom car shows allowed low-riders, hot rods, and other custom cars to sit side by side. Car owners competed for prizes and trophies. At first, not everyone accepted this new breed of car. Some people couldn't understand customizing a car that didn't race or go fast. But in time, they grew to respect lowriders and their amazing machines. They even began to borrow some ideas out of the world of lowriders. A new kind of custom car—the street rod—appeared. The street rod combined features of hot rods and lowriders. Street rods had bigger, more powerful engines. They were usually more expensive than lowriders. Most had fancy accessories and expensive paint jobs.

Little by little, lowriding was entering the American mainstream. It wasn't just a Mexican American trend anymore. Whites, African Americans, and people of almost any race could be seen riding low and slow. In time, the culture even spread to Europe and Japan.

During the 1960s, the Impala (especially the 1964 Impala) became the classic model for a lowrider. The Impala, like the early Chevy Deluxe, was sleek and inexpensive. But lowriding wasn't limited to just

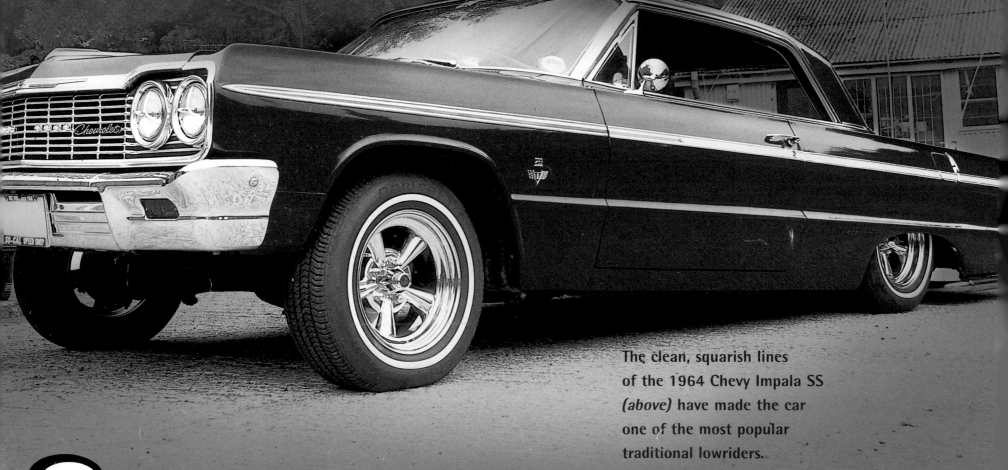

The clean, squarish lines of the 1964 Chevy Impala SS (*above*) have made the car one of the most popular traditional lowriders.

cars anymore. Some owners started customizing lowrider trucks and even lowrider motorcycles and bicycles.

Scraping

In the late 1960s, a new sport came out of lowriding—scrape racing. If lowriders drove their cars really low, the metal bottoms of their cars dragged on the pavement. This scraping metal left a bright trail of sparks. Some drivers liked the effect. They would scrape down the road on purpose. And if one car scraping was cool, two cars racing side by side was even better.

Scraping was very hard on the cars. Replacing damaged parts was expensive. So drivers welded steel blocks, called scrape plates, to the bottom of their cars. Using scrape plates, the drivers could scrape and spark away without damaging their cars.

Lowriding had always been about looks and style, not speed. Scraping was no exception. Drivers tried new alloys (combinations of metals) for their scrape plates. They discovered plates that gave more and brighter sparks—even colored sparks.

Lowrider motorcycles *(above)* are a cool way to enjoy the style of lowriders on two or three wheels.

Scrape racing wasn't the only developing lowrider sport. New, powerful hydraulic systems led to "hopping" and "dancing" competitions. These exciting events have pushed the limits of hydraulics to a new test.

The controversial movie *Boulevard Nights* portrayed lowriders as criminals.

Everything happens on the boulevard— and the boulevard happens at night.

BOULEVARD NIGHTS

A TONY BILL/BILL BENENSON PRODUCTION
"BOULEVARD NIGHTS" Starring RICHARD YÑIGUEZ · MARTA DUBOIS · DANNY DE LA PAZ
Directed by MICHAEL PRESSMAN · Produced by BILL BENENSON · Executive Producer TONY BILL
Written by DESMOND NAKANO · Music by LALO SCHIFRIN · Song "STREET TATTOO" · Performed by GEORGE BENSO[N]
TECHNICOLOR® ©Copyright 1979 Warner Bros. Inc. All Rights Reserved. Original Soundtrack on Warner Bros. Records and
DISTRIBUTED BY WARNER BROS. [W] A WARNER COMMUNICATIONS COMPANY

A Changing Culture

By the late 1970s, lowriding had come a long way. But the release of the 1979 movie *Boulevard Nights* set the hobby back again. The movie featured criminal street gangs and their lowrider cars on the famous Whittier Boulevard in Los Angeles. *Boulevard Nights* caused some people to think that lowriding had strong connections to criminal gangs. Again, lowriders had trouble finding good places to cruise. Favorite spots like Whittier Boulevard were off-limits.

Whittier Boulevard

For years Los Angeles's Whittier Boulevard was the most popular cruise strip, or street to cruise. But by the 1970s, violence and crime was giving the street—and lowriding— a bad name. People called lowrider clubs "gangs on wheels." In the early 1980s, police closed the boulevard to cruisers.

Dancing and hopping competitions, such as the one shown here, had become a regular part of lowrider shows by the 1970s. This is a 1964 Chevy Impala SS.

Again, lowriders turned to car shows as a way of gathering to show off their creations. Soon a split in the lowriding community appeared. Some owners were building lowriders just for show. They loaded the cars in trailers to move them around. They never drove them on the road. One group of owners didn't think this was right—lowriders were meant to be driven. The lines between "street lowriders" and "show lowriders" were drawn. Car shows became the battlegrounds. The debate of "show versus go" lives on.

How an Internal Combustion Engine Works

Like most cars, lowriders have internal combustion engines. They run on gasoline and use a four-stroke cycle *(right)*. The four-stroke cycle burns a mixture of air and gas to power the car. These cycles take place thousands of times per minute inside a car engine. In the early days of lowriding, engines were not important. Looks were the key. But many modern lowriders want their cars to have both looks and speed. So powerful engines have grown in popularity in recent years.

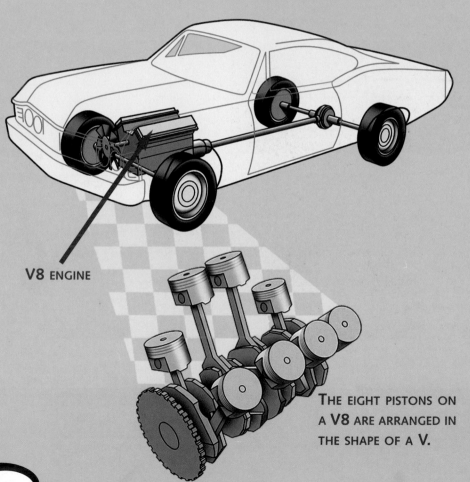

V8 ENGINE

THE EIGHT PISTONS ON A **V8** ARE ARRANGED IN THE SHAPE OF A **V.**

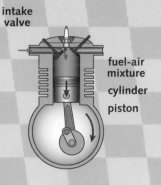

intake valve

fuel-air mixture

cylinder

piston

1. INTAKE STROKE
The piston moves down the cylinder and draws the fuel-air mixture into the cylinder through the intake valve.

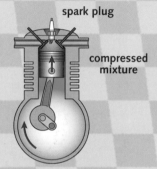

spark plug

compressed mixture

2. COMPRESSION STROKE
The piston moves up and compresses the fuel-air mixture. The spark plug ignites the mixture, creating combustion (burning).

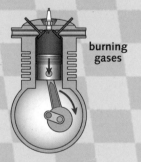

burning gases

3. POWER STROKE
The burning gases created by combustion push the piston downward. This gives the engine its power.

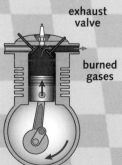

exhaust valve

burned gases

4. EXHAUST STROKE
The piston moves up again and pushes out the burned-out exhaust gases through the exhaust valve.

Lowriding continued to branch out in the 1980s and 1990s. The old idea of using only inexpensive, used cars was long gone. Lowriders made dream machines out of trucks, European cars, Japanese cars, and even sports cars. At first, many classic lowrider owners rejected these new types. How could they be judged against bombs and traditionals? But the answer was simple—lowriding needed a class system for car shows. Suddenly, there was room for everyone. Again, the hobby had undergone a big change, and again, it was stronger because of it. All of these new ideas and events have kept lowriders fresh and exciting in the 2000s.

A lowrider shows off the hydraulic system of his 1967 Cadillac Coupe DeVille. The box he is holding has switches that control the pumps that lift and lower the car's wheels.

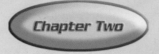
LOWRIDER CULTURE

Lowriding is bigger than ever. It's a hobby and a passion that blends a love of cars with craftsmanship and artistic expression. Owners spend time and money on their lowriders out of the pure love of customizing a car (or truck, bike, or motorcycle) that expresses their personality.

Classic lowriders, or bombs, remain popular. But in recent decades, new, bolder lowrider designs have grown in popularity. The range of car models used as lowriders has exploded. Any kind of vehicle—minivans, limousines, even hearses—are fair game.

The types of customizations owners give their lowriders have changed as well. Early lowrider customizations focused mainly on the cars' exterior.

Over time, they began to give the interior the same kind of attention. They replaced the car's fabric and carpeting with plush velvet and velour fabrics. They added chrome fixtures, fancy bucket seats, small steering wheels, and window blinds. The wildest rides have features such as televisions and fish tanks.

Hydraulics

After Ron Aguirre introduced hydraulics in 1959, lowrider culture changed forever. Hydraulic systems became a huge part of the lowriding experience. In fact, most people don't even consider a car to be a lowrider unless it has a hydraulic system.

For many, lowriding is a family tradition. Love of lowrider cars and culture is handed down from generation to generation.

Lowrider
Hydraulic Systems

A lowrider's hydraulic system is attached to the suspension of the car. (The suspension is the parts that connect the wheels to the basic frame of the car.) The pumps raise or lower the hydraulic cylinder, causing the car's body to go up or down. The hydraulic system is attached to a set of switches that the driver controls.

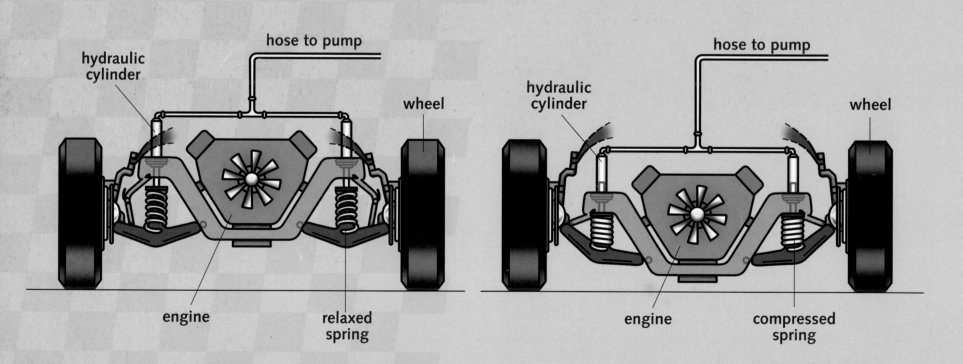

RAISED POSITION

hose to pump

hydraulic cylinder

wheel

engine

relaxed spring

LOWERED POSITION

hose to pump

hydraulic cylinder

wheel

engine

compressed spring

Pumps are the center of a hydraulic system. The pumps hold the fluid and provide the power that forces that fluid into the cylinders attached to each wheel. When the pumps fill the cylinders, the car is raised. To lower the lowrider, the pumps release pressure. This allows the fluid to flow out of the cylinders into a "dump," where it is stored.

Hydraulic pumps use a lot of energy. The car's normal battery can't handle the heavy load. So lowriders often have a large bank of heavy-duty batteries in the trunk. Some cars can have ten or more batteries in the trunk just to power the hydraulic pumps.

As with most lowriders, the plush trunk of this 1967 Cadillac contains both pumps and batteries. The pumps are the shiny chrome parts in the middle of the trunk. The banks of black batteries are set along the sides.

For some lowriders, there is no such thing as too much chrome. This piece of automotive art even has a chrome plated suspension system. This car is a 1964 Chevy Impala.

Chrome and Paint Jobs

Most lowrider owners value looks above all else. They'll do almost anything to make their lowriders sleeker and more eye-catching.

Chrome plating is one of the most popular options. This process makes any metal part look like new, shining silver. Owners add chrome to the car's interior, fenders, and metal trim.

Some who build lowriders for show even add chrome plating to the entire engine, making everything under the hood shine.

Custom paint jobs are also popular. Many lowriders have "candy" paint jobs. Adding layers of lacquer—a clear, shiny coating—over the paint makes the cars shine like new. Bombs usually have simple, single-color paint jobs without much decoration. But many traditionals and modern lowriders have detailed, multicolor paint jobs. Stripes, swirls, and other bright patterns are common. Coats upon coats of lacquer give the cars the showroom shine that almost all owners prize.

Many types of cars have fancy paint jobs. But murals are a special lowrider trait. Owners often paint these unique images on the hood or the side of the cars. But they can be painted on any panel. Religious icons are among the most popular murals. Images from the Bible, such as the Virgin Mary and Jesus, appear on many lowriders.

Some owners add self-portraits or images of family members. Others feature images of moments in history. Famous people are also popular. Cesar Chavez, a leader for Mexican American farmworkers during the 1960s and 1970s, appears on many lowriders. Some murals are meant to be light and funny—cartoon characters, wild monsters, and ghosts. Almost anything goes.

Women and Lowriding

Women have built some award-winning lowriders. They include Sandra Velo's 1971 Buick Riviera, named *Chola One*, Linda Lopez's 1947 Chevy Fleetmaster, *Golden Dream*, and Ami Fukawa's 1963 Impala, *Lady's Touch*.

The hood of this 1949 Buick features flame detailing and a brilliant mural.

Many lowriders have soft, plush, and colorful interiors. This slick machine even has a TV in the dashboard.

Accessories

The accessories on a lowrider are almost as important as its hydraulics and paint job. Owners love customizing their lowriders with eye-catching additions.

A lowrider's interior gives owners all kinds of options for adding accessories. Replacing the car's steering wheel is an easy change. Many owners add small steering wheels made of welded chain links. These chrome-plated "fat man" wheels get their name from the extra room they provide for heavier drivers.

Plush interior fabrics and carpeting are a must for many newer lowriders. Owners tear out the factory seats and fabric. Then they replace them with cushioned bucket seats covered in soft velvet and velour fabrics. Often they even cover the paneling, roof, and dash in the same fabric. Soft matching carpets complete the look.

Early lowriders focused on the car's exterior. That tradition lives on. Exterior accessories include chrome bumpers and fenders, fog lights, bumper guards, and more. Old-fashioned air conditioners called swamp coolers are a popular accessory on bombs.

These devices were popular before modern air-conditioning systems were widely available. A swamp cooler looks like a large tube that hangs out one of the rear windows. It cools the car by evaporating water. Windshield visors, sirens, special hubcaps, and car club plaques are other common exterior accessories.

A chain-link fat man steering wheel *(above)*. The large air-conditioning tube attached to the side of this 1947 Pontiac Sedan Coupe *(below)* is known as a swamp cooler.

No lowrider is complete without a booming sound system. The subwoofers *(the two round speakers along the back of the trunk)* in this Mercedes sedan can really pump up the volume.

For some owners, the most important accessory is the sound system. They add big CD changers (which usually go in the trunk) and huge speaker systems. The biggest systems can have 20 speakers or more. The sound system usually centers on the subwoofers. These large speakers are designed to pump out heavy bass (low) notes that are so powerful that they can rattle the entire car. For these owners, lowriding isn't just about being seen—it's also about being *heard*.

Hopping and Dancing

Most people come to shows to check out the stunning paint jobs, plush interiors, and big sound systems. But the key events for any lowrider show are the two lowrider sports, "hopping" and "dancing."

Hopping competitions are simple. Owners equip their cars with the most powerful hydraulic pumps they can find. A quick burst of fluid to the front cylinders raises the car so fast that the front tires hop off the ground.

Officials measure how far the car's wheels come up and award prizes to the owners of the cars with the highest marks. Hopping takes place in several classes, including Single-Pump Car, Double-Pump Car, Truck Hop, Luxury Hop, and Radical Hop. Some cars can get their front tires 6 feet (2 meters) or more off the ground.

Dancing competitions are set to music. Owners use independently controlled hydraulics (the cylinder for each wheel is controlled separately).

Dancing competitions like this one are some of the most exciting and popular events at lowrider shows. The car below is a 1964 Chevy Impala Sport Coupe.

Lowrider Bikes

Some young people can't wait until they're old enough to drive to get started with lowriding. So they customize their bikes. They drop the frames low to the ground, add plush seats, fancy wheels, fat man steering wheels, and other accessories. They even add chrome to the bike's metal. Lowrider bikes are a great way for kids and adults to express themselves and show their skills and craftsmanship. The lowrider bike above features twisted metal, a spare tire with a plush cover, a mural along the frame, a chrome headlight, whitewall tires, big rearview mirrors, and more.

They make the car jump, bob, and rock to the music. Judges score each lowrider's dancing routine. The judges' scores are based on the quality and difficulty of the moves and on how well the dance fits the music. Dancing classes include Street Car Dance, Street Truck Dance, and Radical Dance.

Classes

Lowrider shows feature dozens—sometimes hundreds—of prizes. Individual awards honor the best interior, the best mural, the best engine, and more. Lowriders are split into dozens of classes, including bombs, originals, radicals, full customs, and luxury cars. The top overall prize is Lowrider of the Year.

One of the newer lowrider classes is the Euro class. This includes any small imported car—and not just cars from Europe. Japanese cars also compete in the Euro class. In fact, two

of the most popular Euro models are the Toyota Celica and Nissan Maxima. Another popular Euro lowrider model is the Volkswagen Beetle (also called the Bug). The Beetle helped bring Euros into the lowriding mainstream.

While many lowriders rejected these new models and classes at first, most have come to accept them. The old days when lowriders were just big American cars have passed. The new owners bring a fresh dose of fun to the hobby. Lowriding started out as a way to make inexpensive cars look great. That tradition lives on with Euros.

Mercedes-Benzes, like this one, are popular choices for high-end Euro class cars.

This metal body model of a 1964 Chevy Impala SS lowrider was built from a Revell kit.

Lowrider Modeling

Cars, motorcycles, and bicycles aren't the only forms of lowrider art. Some lowriders show off their skills by making incredible plastic or die-cast metal models. Model kit-makers such as Revell-Monogram sell highly detailed kits of many award-winning lowrider cars. Lowriders young and old can assemble these models from the wheels up. Modelers can follow the instructions to make the car look just like the original lowrider the kit is based on. Or they can be creative and paint and style the car to make a one-of-a-kind masterpiece.

More ambitious modelers will start with models of non-lowrider cars. They will customize the kits to turn the model from a normal car into a lowrider. They might lower the body, turn the doors into suicide doors, and add totally wild paint jobs. Some modelers even make tiny hydraulic systems for their model cars.

Lowriding has come a long way since the days when Mexican Americans put bags of sand or blocks of cement in their trunks to lower their cars. The hobby has created an industry with its very own parts suppliers, customizers, network of lowrider shows, and magazines. Lowriding has grown from the barrios of Los Angeles to spread across the world. With so many creative and skilled people doing so many cool things, lowriding can only continue to grow as a popular hobby.

A group of lowriders pose with their prized possessions. The car in front is a 1954 Chevrolet. The car behind it to the right is a 1956 Chevrolet.

1947 Pontiac Fastback

This car is an excellent example of a classic bomb. The car itself is a big, roomy Pontiac coupe with a slick, rounded shape. The back end of the car slopes down from the roof to the bumper in a style known as a fast-back. It has many of the accessories seen on bombs. They include a swamp cooler for air conditioning, windshield visor, headlight visors, small wheels, whitewall tires, and foglights on the sides and on the front grille.

1949 Buick Fastback, *Fireball*

This fastback bomb has been heavily customized. The car's bodywork has been sculpted to make the rear fenders extra long and wide. The roof has been chopped—it has been lowered to make the car look lower and meaner. Note the rear taillights, which stick out of the fenders like jets of flame. A flaming paint job is what gives this car its name. Like many bombs, this lowrider has floodlights and a windshield visor.

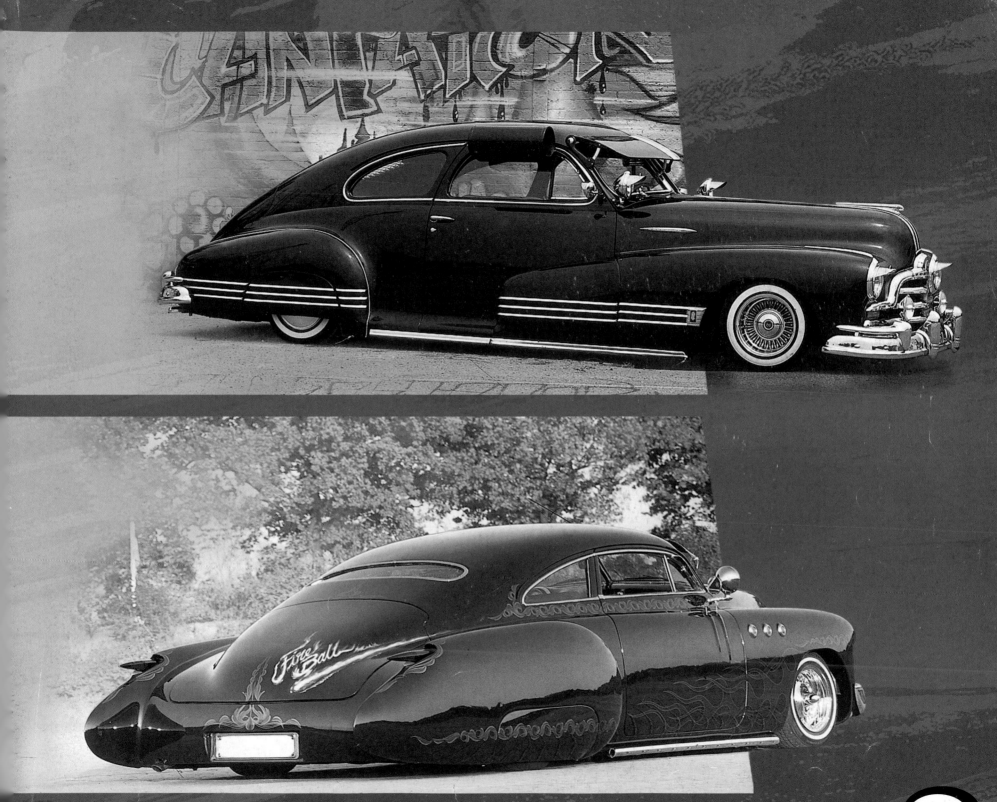

1958 Chevy Impala

This car is a classic traditional *(facing page)*. Chevys from the 1950s are some of the most popular cars among lowriders, hot-rodders, and many other classic car collectors. They are big, have great looks, and many come equipped with powerful V8 engines *(right)*. This lowrider's owner has given his car a clean look. He has customized the front grille, adding slick horizontal chrome bars. Gray custom stripes create a vivid paint job.

1959 Chevy Impala Hearse

Here's a wild idea. Take an old Chevy hearse, and turn it into a slick monster lowrider. People have said the 1959 Impala's spooky tail end *(facing page)* looks like an angry Martian or a smiling cat. This mean machine has tough-looking spikes on its front grille *(right)*. Large, slick chrome wheel rims and extra thin tires give the car an extra low ride. This machine even has a supercharger sticking out of the hood that provides extra speed to get customers to the cemetery fast.

1964 Chevy Impala SS *Latin Style*

This traditional belongs to Pete Salas of the Los Padrinos lowriders club of Saint Paul, Minnesota. Pete's ride features mirrored head-lamps and a hand-painted mural *(facing page)* of an Aztec warrior on the hood. Several layers of clearcoat lacquer give the car's multicolored metal flake paint an incredible shine.

1966 Chevy Impala

This lowrider is showing off its hydraulics *(right)*. Nearly all lowriders have independent suspensions. This means that each wheel can move up and down on its own. These systems allow lowriders to raise or lower one, two, three, or all wheels at the same time or sepa-rately. A look at the colorful plush trunk *(facing page)* shows the amazing detail and craftsmanship that goes into so many lowriders.

1966 Pontiac Tempest GTO

Sometimes a simple look can make for a very cool lowrider. The creator of this car went with a simple key lime body color. Then he accented it with touches of white marble on the bumpers and headlight fairings. The attractive color combination extends to the interior *(right)*, which features white and black leather seats and a green dash. The small box on the seat is the hydraulics controller. The side-opening hood and trunk *(facing page)* add some extra flair to a beautiful machine.

1985 Pontiac Grand Prix *Sweet 'n Sour*

The Pontiac Grand Prix and Chevy Monte Carlo are popular choices for many lowriders. Models from the 1980s have a clean, squarish shape that many people like. This car is named *Sweet 'n Sour*. Its brilliant flecked orange and red paint scheme looks like reddish orange sweet and sour sauce. The owner of this car has added plenty of gold details, including gold bumpers and gold wheels. As the picture on the facing page shows, this car's hydraulic system is fully functional.

1985 Dodge
Heavy-Duty Pickup Truck

This lowrider was customized by Rayvern Hydraulics in Great Britain. It's a deep purple Dodge pickup *(facing page)* that will get you to the beach for surfing in style. Chrome-plated hydraulic pumps *(right)* don't just raise and lower the wheels. A pump is also hooked up to the cargo bed tops for stylish loading and unloading. The truck's body has been smoothed to perfection, and the rear bumper has been removed to create a cleaner look.

1987 Chevy Astro Minivan

This lowrider van *(facing page)* is another Rayvern Hydraulics creation. Rayvern uses this Astro minivan to travel to and from car shows. The company specializes in making hydraulics for lowriders and has created some incredible machines over the years. A minivan is an unusual choice for a lowrider, but the Chevy Astro is a perfect fit because its skirt *(bottom of the body)* is the same height all the way around. The van's wild paint job really captures people's attention.

Volkswagen (VW) Beetle

The VW Beetle has long been a favorite car of Euro class lowriders. This Rayvern creation has a ton of wild customizations. The front and rear bumpers have been removed for a smoother look. The cracks between fenders and main body have also been smoothed over. The convertible roof has been chopped to give the car a lower look. Finally, the doors and trunk (where the engine sits in a Beetle) have been changed to open in unusual ways *(facing page)*.

Volkswagen Transporter Van

The VW van was a popular vehicle in the United States in the 1960s. This Euro class lowrider sports a vivid silver and orange paint scheme, extrawide rims, and thin tires. Tinted windows keep the hot sun out and add to the car's cool look.

Glossary

bomb: a lowrider model made before 1958

chrome: a coating of a metallic substance called chromium that gives metal objects a shiny, new look

customize: to change a vehicle's appearance

Euro: a lowrider class of small, imported cars, mainly from Europe and Japan

hot rod: a type of car customized for both looks and speed

hydraulics: a system of pumps that force fluid into cylinders to lift heavy objects

lacquer: a clear coating that is applied over a car's paint. Lacquer gives the paint a shiny "candy" appearance.

mural: a themed painting on a lowrider

rim: the outer part of the wheel

street rod: a type of car that combines features of hot rods and lowriders

traditional: a lowrider model made between 1959 and the mid-1970s

zoot suit: a style of dress that started in urban African American communities and became popular among young Mexican American men during the late 1930s and 1940s. Zoot suits featured oversized coats and high-waisted, baggy pants.

Selected Bibliography

Genat, Robert. *Lowriders*. Saint Paul, MN: Motorbooks International, 2003.

Lowrider magazine editors. *The Lowrider's Handbook*. New York: HPBooks, 2002.

Penland, Paige A. *Lowriders: History, Pride, Culture*. Saint Paul, MN: Motorbooks International, 2003.

Further Reading

Abraham, Philip. *Cars*. New York: Children's Press, 2004.

Maurer, Tracy. *Lowriders*. Vero Beach, FL: Rourke Publishing, 2004.

Parr, Ann. *Lowriders*. Philadelphia: Chelsea House, 2005.

Websites

The BumpStop
> http://www.bumpstop.com
> Bumpstop is a center for custom car enthusiasts. It features photo galleries, car club listings, and news.

Los Padrinos
> http://www.lospadrinos.com/home_page.htm
> Check out pictures of cool lowrider cars and bikes at the website of this Saint Paul, Minnesota-based, lowrider club.

Index

About the Author

Matt Doeden is a freelance author and editor living in Minnesota. He has written more than 50 children's books, including dozens on cars and drivers.

About the Consultant

Pete Salas is the founder of Los Padrinos (the Godfathers), a Saint Paul, Minnesota-based, lowrider club that is a member of the National Lowrider Club Registry. He is the owner of a 1964 Chevy Impala SS lowrider.

Photo Acknowledgments